Stones Rolled Away and Other Addresses

by Henry Drummond

Wilder Publications, LLC.
PO Box 3005
Radford VA 24143-3005

ISBN 10: 1-60459-184-6
ISBN 13: 978-1-60459-184-2

Table of Contents

Introduction

Any one who had read "The Greatest Thing in the World" could not help but desire to see and hear its author; and, when Professor Drummond visited Boston in the spring of 1893, the capacity of lecture halls was taxed to the utmost. To accommodate thousands turned away, he repeated some of his lectures in the Lowell Institute Course, Boston. It was a crowded Boylston Hall or Appleton Chapel that invariably faced him when he addressed the students of Harvard University. He drew young men as few men can. He loved life and nature. He studied and knew men. He had read much. He had travelled in Europe, America, Africa, Australia and the New Hebrides, with eyes and ears wide open. With a charming personality and a rare grace of manner, he was a most attractive speaker and character, whether on the platform or in the quiet hour.

The student, the evangelist and pastor, the professor and lecturer, the traveller and writer, has passed away; but his words, his writing and his influence cannot. He willingly gave his life to help others. Many a soul was brought into a higher life. Many a life was led into the top flat. Many a one was shown his part in the Kingdom of God. Many a man who was down was set upon his feet. Many a stone of difficulty was rolled away.

The addresses here given to the public in permanent form for the first time, as they have already helped some, may yet help many more.

The first four were delivered to students of Harvard University, in April, 1893. The remaining three addresses were delivered at the World's Bible Students' Conference, Northfield, Mass., in July, 1893.

Luther Hess Waring
Scranton, PA.

Stones Rolled Away

Gentlemen, I am very much astonished at this spectacle. I told you last night it was against our principles in Scotland to have religious meetings on a week night. It seems to me that if you come to a meeting of this kind you mean business, and you may just as well own it. If a man comes to a shorthand class, it means that he wants to learn shorthand; and, if a man turns up at what I suppose I must call a religious meeting, it means that he is less or more interested in the subject.

Now I should say that I think a man has to give himself the benefit of that desire, and he should not be ashamed of it. The facts of religion are real; and, as mere students of life, you and I are bound to take cognizance of them. Of course, many very fair minded men are kept away from going into this subject as they would like by a number of exceedingly surface reasons. I cannot help calling them surface reasons. For instance, you meet a man who tells you that he doesn't like Christians, that they always put his back up.

Now, Christians often put my back up. There are many of them I find, with whom it takes all my time to get along. But that is not peculiar with Christians. It is only peculiar to peculiar Christians, and there are just as many of the other sort. A man might just as well say, I don't like sinners. A man might just as well keep out of the world because he doesn't like some people in the world, as to keep out of Christian circles because there are some objectionable creatures in it. We cannot be too fastidious. We cannot join any sect without having the weaker brethren in it. We cannot get on in this world entirely by ourselves. We must join this thing and that if we are going to be of any service at all, so that I think the difficulty of having to join ourselves with objectionable men applies pretty much all around.

Other men are kept away from Christianity by what I might call its phrases. A great many people, not so much in your country as in ours, talk in a dialect. The older people especially, our grandmothers, have a set of phrases in which all their religion is imbedded, and they can't talk to us about religion without using those phrases; and when we talk to them, if we do not use those phrases, we are put out of the synagogue. Now what we can do in this case is to translate their dialect into our own language, and then translate into their dialect when we speak back. It is a different dialect. We would put it upon a different basis; but after all we mean pretty much the same thing, and if we can once get into this habit of translating our more modern way of putting things into this antique language that those worthy people use to us we will find ourselves more at one with them than we think.

I meet another set of men who tell me that they don't like churches, that they find sermons stale, flat and unprofitable. Now, if any man here hates a dull sermon, I am with him. I have intense sympathy with any man who hates dullness. I think the world is far too dull, and that is one of the greatest reasons why the brightest men should throw themselves into Christianity to give it a broader phase to other people. One must confess that some church work, at all events, is not of a very cheerful or lively order. But of course that is not an argument why one should abstain from religious service. There are many reasons why we should even sacrifice ourselves and submit to a little dullness now and again if it is going to gain for us a greater good. After all, we live by institutions, and by fixed institutions. There are very few men who are able to get along without steady institutions of one kind and another. Some men are so tremendously free that they hate to be tied down to hours, to places and to seasons; but there are very few men big enough to stand that for a long time. If we look about for it, we will find some place that we can go and get some good. When a man goes to church really hungry and goes because he is hungry, he will pick up something, no matter where it is. Christ himself went to church, and even if we know something more than the minister knows, the fellowship, the sense of the solidarity of the Christian church throughout the whole world, the prayer and the inspiration of the hymn and the reading will at least do us some good. I do not say that a man cannot be very religious without that. There are tens of thousands of Christians who never go to church; and there are tens of thousands who go to church who are not Christians. But, as with substantial meals taken at intervals, man is no worse and may be much better for it.

The religious life needs keeping up just as the other parts of our life need keeping up. There is nothing more impossible than for a man to live a religious life on an hour's work or an hour's thought a week. A man could not learn French, German or Latin by giving an hour per week to it; and how can we expect a man to get in this great world of the spirit, this great moral world, this great ideal region, and learn anything about it by merely dabbling in it now and again? We must make it a regular business, and, if the religious part is a vital part of the whole nature, we may as well attend to it.

You may remember a passage in Mr. Darwin's life. He says: "In one respect my mind has changed during the last twenty or thirty years. Up to the age of thirty, or beyond it, the poetry of many kinds, such as the works of Milton, Gray, Byron, Coleridge and Shelley, gave me great pleasure; and even as a school boy I took intense delight in Shakespeare, and especially in the historical plays. I have always said that pictures gave me considerable, and music very great, delight. But now for many years I cannot endure to read a line of poetry. I have tried lately to read Shakespeare, but found it so intolerably dull that it nauseated me. I have also lost my taste for pictures and music. My mind seems to have become a kind of machine for grinding general laws out of large collections of facts. But why this should have caused the atrophy of that part of the brain, I cannot conceive. If I had my life to live over again" (this is the point) "I would have made the rule to read some poetry and listen to some music at least once every week." There is the greatest authority on degeneration confessing to his own personal degeneration, and in the same paragraph telling us how we may avoid it. He says by leaving these things out of his life for so many years, although he had a real liking for them, his nature at these points began to atrophy, and when he went back to them he found that they disgusted him; and then he says that, if he had his life to live again, he would have made it a rule to read some poetry and listen to some music at least once a week, and that would have kept the thing up. There is nothing magical about religion. If a man is to keep it up, he must use the means, just as he would use the means to keep up the violin, or his interest in art of any kind.

I find another set of men who have never got beyond this difficulty, that they find the Bible a somewhat arid and slow book. Now, in the first place, I want to say that I have, again, great sympathy with that objector because, as a matter of fact, there are whole tracts of the Bible which are distinctly dull, which are written in an archaic language, and about departments of history in the past which haven't any great living interest for us now. One must remember that the Bible is not a book, but a library consisting of a large number of books. By an accident, we have these books bound up in one as if they were one book; and to say that all the books of the Bible are dull is simply to pass a literary judgment which is incorrect. It is not true, as a matter of fact, that all these books of the Bible are dull. Of course a sailing directory is very flat on the shore; but when a man is at sea and wants to steer his way through difficult and dangerous wastes, where the currents are strong and the passages narrow, he wants the best chart he can get, and he wants to use it as carefully as he can; and when a man wakens up to the difficulty of life and the reality of its temptations, he wants some such chart as he gets in that book to help him through.

As a mere literary work, there are books there that are unsurpassed in the English tongue, and for their teaching, for their beauty and for their truth they have never been surpassed. Christ's words, of course, are beyond comparison; but even Paul had a far greater brain than almost any writer of history.

John's writing is far deeper and more beautiful than Emerson's, for instance. Let the man who is in love with Emerson, as I am happy to say I am, take up the book of John just as he would take up Emerson, and see if he doesn't get in it a great deal that Emerson has, and a great deal more. If a man doesn't like the Bible, it is because he has never struck the best parts of it, or because he has never felt any great need in his own life for its teaching. As a matter of fact, however, reading the Bible is a new thing. There were Christians for hundreds and hundreds of years before there was any people's Bible; so that it is not even essential, if you can't overcome this matter of taste, that you should read the Bible. There are hundreds of Christians at this moment who cannot read the Bible. There are Christians in heathen lands in whose language there is as yet no Bible; so that you see there is no absolute connection between these two things. Besides that, the Bible has now become diffused through literature to such an extent that you can often get the heart of the Bible in a very bright and living and practical form through other forms of literature. If you don't care to get it direct from the book itself, you can get it from our modern poetry, even from our modern novel; and Christianity has now been so long in the world and is diffused over so many things that it reflects itself in almost everything in life. Some one was once trying to convince a certain lady of that point as they were sitting at dinner; and he said to her that in the pudding which they had just eaten there was an egg, and that that morning at breakfast he had also eaten an egg. He saw the egg at breakfast, but he did not see the egg in the pudding; yet he had no doubt the egg in the pudding would nourish him just as much as the one he had for breakfast.

A man may get his nourishment straight out of the Bible. He may see it there, shell and all; but he may also get his nourishment mixed up with other ingredients, and it will do him just as much good.

There is another class of men, however, whom none of these minor difficulties touch—men who have come up to college, and who have got upset on almost all the main doctrines of Christianity. Now, I want to confess to you that, so far as I know my old friends, they have all passed through that stage. Every man who is worth a button passes through that stage. He loses all the forms of truth which he got in the Sunday School; and, if he is true to himself, gains them all back again in a richer and larger and more permanent form. But, between the loss and the gain, there is sometimes a very painful and dismal interlude, during which the man thinks that he is never going to believe again, when everything lies in ruin, and he doesn't see where any reconstruction is to come in. These are dark days and dark years in a man's life, and they are inevitable to every man who thinks. They are inevitable, because we are all born doubters. We came into the world asking questions. The world itself is a sphinx and tempts us to keep on asking questions. There are no great truths in the world which are not to some extent doubtable; and the instrument with which we look at truth is largely impaired, and has to be corrected by long years of experience for its early aberration. So that when we look at truth we only see part of it, and we see that part of it distorted. The result is a certain amount of twilight where we expected full day. One consolation to give that man is to tell him that we have all been through that. We take it like the measles. It lasts a certain number of months or years, and then we come out with our constitutions better than ever. There is a real rationale for that. Everything in the world passes through these stages, provided it be growing. You remember how the philosophers describe it. They describe the three great stages as position, opposition and composition. Position: Somebody lays down a truth, you look at it and say, "Yes, that is truth." I heard a clergyman say that when I was a boy, and I believed it. Then, one day, you read a book or hear some one else talk, and he put a query on it; and then there came the revolt against it, and for a long time your mind was seething with opposition to this original thing which was positive. And then you went on and put all these contradictory things together and composed them into a unity again. You reached the third stage—that of composition.

It is the same with everything. You begin to learn the piano, and after you have played about a year you think you know all about it; and you tackle the most difficult pieces, dash away at them, and think you can do it as well as anybody. Then you go into Boston and hear some great pianist, and come home a sad man. You see you know nothing about it. For the next six months you do not touch a single piece. You play scales day after day and practice finger exercises. Then, after six months, you say: "What is the use of playing scales? Music does not exist for scales;" and you turn to your old pieces and play them over again in an entirely different way. You have got it all back again. There are men here going through the scale period with regard to religious questions. What is the use of all this opposition? Is it not time to go back again, you ask, and put all this experience into something, and get at some truth at the other side? You see the same truth in a novel. Volume I., they will. Volume II., they won't. Volume III., they do.

We see the same thing in art. A man paints a picture. He thinks he has painted a grand one. After a few months, some one comes along and says: "Look here! Look at that boat! You don't call that a boat? And look at that leaf! That is not a leaf." And you discover that you have never looked at a boat and never seen a leaf. You are disheartened and do nothing the next six months but draw boats and leaves; and, after you have drawn boats and leaves until you are sick, you say: "What is the use of drawing boats and leaves?" and try again and produce your first landscape. But it is altogether a different thing from the picture you painted before. Now, when a man is working over the details of the Christian religion and struggling to get one thing adjusted and another, he will very soon find out that that does not amount to much. It is a useful thing, and he has to go through it, but he has to come out the other side also and put these things together.

The best advice, I think, that can be given to a man who is in this difficulty is, in the first place, to read the best authorities on the subject; not to put himself off with cheap tracts and popular sermons, but to go to the scientific authorities. There are as great scientific authorities in Germany, in England and in America on all the subject matter of theology as there are on the subject matter of chemistry or geology. Go to the authorities. You may not agree with them when you have read them. But if a man reads all the books on the opposition side he will very naturally get a distorted view of it. So, for every book he reads on the one side, he should, in justice, read a book on the other side.

Next, let a man remember that the great thing is not to think about religion, but to do it. We do not live in a "think" world. It is a real world.

You do not believe that botany lies in the pages of Sachs. Botany lies out there in the flowers and in the trees, and it is living. And religion does not live in the pages of the doctrinal books, but in human life—in conflict with our own temptations, and in the conduct and character of our fellow beings. When we abandon this "think-world" of ours and get out into the real world, we will find that, after all, these doubts are not of such immense importance, and that we can do a great deal of good in the world.

For my part, I have as many doubts on all the great subjects connected with theology as probably any one here; but they do not interfere in the very slightest with my trying, in what humble way I can, to follow out the religion of Christ. They do not even touch that region; and I don't want to lose these doubts. I don't want any man to rob me of my problem. I have no liking and little respect for the cock-sure Christian—a man who can demonstrate some of the most tremendous verities of the faith, as he can the Fifth Book of Euclid. I want a religion and theology with some of the infinite about it, and some of the shadow as well as some of the light; and if, by reading up one of the great doctrines for five or six years, I get some little light upon it, it is only to find there are a hundred upon which I could spend another hundred lives. And if I should try to meet some specific point upon which you are at sea to-night, it would not do you much good. To-morrow a new difficulty would start in your mind, and you would be simply where you were. I would be stopping up only one of your wells. You would open another out of the first book you read. Try to separate theological doctrine from practical religion. Believe me that you can follow Christ in this University without having solved any of these problems. Why, there was a skeptic among the first twelve disciples, and one of the best of them, and one of the most loyal of them. That man sat down at the first Lord's table, and Christ never said any hard words against him. He tried to teach him. That is the only attitude, it seems to me, we can take to Christ still. We can enter His school as scholars, and sit at His feet and learn what we can; and by doing His will in the practical things of life, we shall know of this and that doctrine, whether it be of God. The only use of truth is that it can do somebody some good. The only use of truth is in its sanctifying power; and that is the peculiarity of the truth of Christianity, that it has this sanctifying power and makes men better.

Now you say: "What am I to do? If I am to block up this avenue and am not to expect very much along the line of mere belief, in what direction am I to shape my Christian life?" Well, I cannot in the least answer that. Every man must shape his Christian life for himself, according as his own talents may lead him; but the great thing to do is simply to become a follower of Christ. That is to become a Christian. There is nothing difficult or mysterious about it. A Darwinian is a man who follows Darwin, studies his books, accepts his views and says, "I am a Darwinian." You look into Christ's life, into His influence; you look at the needs of the world; you see how the one meets the other; you look into your own life and see how Christ's life meets your life; and you say, "I shall follow this teacher and leader until I get a better." From the time you do that, you are a Christian. You may be a very poor one. A man who enlists is a very poor soldier for the first few years, but he is a soldier from the moment he enlists; and the moment a man takes Christ to be the center of his life that man becomes a Christian. Of course that makes a great change in his life. His friends will know it to-morrow. On the steam engine you have seen the apparatus at the side called the eccentric. It has a different center from all the other wheels. Now, the Christian man is to some extent an eccentric. His life revolves around a different center from many people round about him. Of course, it is the other people who are eccentric because the true center of life is the most perfect life, the most perfect man, the most perfect ideal; and the man who is circulating around that is living the most perfect. At the same time, that man's life will to some extent be different from the lives round about him, and to some extent he will be a marked man.

But what difference will it make to a man himself? For one thing, it will keep you straight. I fancy most of the men here are living straight lives as it is; but it is impossible that every man here is. Well, I will tell you how to keep your life straight from this time—how your hunger after righteousness can be met. If you become a Christian, you will lead a straight life. That is not all. If you become a Christian, you will help other men to lead straight lives. Seek first the kingdom of God and His righteousness. The only chance that this world has of becoming a righteous world is by the contagion of the Christian men in it. I do not know any country with the splendid pretensions and achievements of America where there is so much unrighteousness in politics and to some extent in commerce, and where shady things are not only winked at, but admired. That is acknowledged and deplored by every right thinking man in the country. I get it, not from observation, but from yourselves. There is not a day passes that I do not find men deploring political corruption and the want of commercial integrity, in some districts of this country, at all events. Now nothing can change that state of affairs unless such men as yourselves throw your influence on to the side of righteousness and determine that you will live to make this country a little straighter than you found it.

There is a career in Christianity as well as an individual life. How do you test the greatness of a career? You test it by its influence. Well, can you point me to any influence in the world in the past which has had anything like the influence of the name to which I have asked you to give your life's adherence? That life started without a chance of succeeding in anything, according to the received theories of a successful life. Christ was born in a manger. If you and I had been born in a manger, the shame of it would have accompanied us through our whole lives; and yet there is not one of us born to-day who is not baptized in the name of Christ and who has not a Christian name. Christ went to no university, and had no education; and there is not a university in Europe or in America which is not founded in the name of Christ. This university was founded in the name of Christ. Aye, and the very money which has gone to build the universities of the world has come from the followers of Christ. The education of the world, gentlemen, has been done by the followers of Jesus Christ. Christ had no political influence, and sought none; yet there is not a President placed in the White House, there is not a sovereign in Europe placed upon a throne, but acknowledges, in the doing of it and in public, that the power to do it has come from Christ, and that the object in doing it is to secure the coming of Christ's kingdom. Take it in any direction, and you will find that this influence, judged from mere worldly standards of success, has been supreme.

Napoleon said, "I do not understand that man. He must have been more than human. I used to be able," he said on St. Helena, "to get people to die for me. I got hundreds of thousands of them, but I had to be there. Now that I am here on this island, I can't get a man. But He," said he, "gets hundreds of thousands of the best men in the world to lay down their whole lives for Him every day." Judged as mere influence from the standpoint of an ambitious man like Napoleon, you see that that Life was supreme.

You remember the dinner that Charles Lamb gave to some literary men, and how they were discussing after dinner what their attitude would be if certain great figures of the past were to come into their dining room. After they had all spoken, Lamb said:

"Well, it looks to me like this, that if Shakespeare entered the room I should rise up to greet him; but if Christ entered the room, I should kneel down and keep silent."

And so I ask you if you have feelings of that kind about any figure in history compared to the feelings that spring into your mind when you try to contemplate that Life. Some of you have never read Christ's life. You have picked up a parable here and a miracle there, and a scrap of history between; but you have never read that biography as you have read the biography of Washington, Webster, or the life of Columbus. Read it. Go home and read one of the four little books which tell you about His life. Take Matthew, for instance; and if you don't run aground in the 5th chapter and find yourself compelled to spend a week over it, you haven't much moral nature left. I have known men who have tried that experiment, who have begun to read the gospel of Matthew, and by the time they had finished reading the 5th chapter, they had thrown in their lot with the Person who forms the subject of that book. There is no other way of getting to know about Christ unless you read His life, at least as a beginning. If you want to become a Christian you must read up, and that is the thing to read. If you like, after that you can read the other lives of Christ. How do men get to know one another? They simply take to one another. Two men meet here to-night. They go downstairs and exchange greetings. To-morrow night they meet in each other's rooms. By the end of a month they have got to know each other a little, and after another year of college life they have become sworn friends.

A man becomes a little attracted to Christ. That grows and grows, into a brighter friendship, and that grows into a great passion, and the man gives his life to Christ's interest. He counts it the highest ambition he can have to become a man such as Christ was. You see there is nothing profound about a religion of that kind. It is a religion that lies in the line of the ideals a young man forms, and that all the reading that he meets with from day to day fashions. In fact, it is a man's ideal turning up, and the man who turns his back upon that is simply turning his back upon his one chance of happiness in life and of making anything off life. Every life that is not lived in that time is out of the true current of history, to say nothing else. It is out of the stream —the main stream that is running through the ages, and that is going to sweep everything before it. A man who does not live that life may not be a bad man. The Bible does not say that everybody who is not a Christian is a notorious sinner; but it says that the man who lives outside that is wasting his life. He may not be doing wrong, but his life is lost. "He that loveth his life," Christ said, "shall lose it; and he that hateth his life in this world shall keep it unto life eternal." I am not ashamed to quote that to you; and I ask you to regard it with the same validity, and more, that you will give to any other quotation.

You will not accuse me of cant because I have used sacred words in this talk. There are technical terms in religion just as in science and philosophy. Just as in science I should speak of protoplasm, of oxygen or carbonic acid gas, so in talking of religion I must talk about faith and Jesus Christ. Just as I should quote authorities in speaking of chemistry or political economy, so I must use authorities in speaking about Christ. You will not take the words that I have said tonight as a mere expression of phraseology of a cant description, because it is not that; and I would ask those of you who are very much frightened to use such words to consider whether it is not a rational thing and a necessary thing, if you speak at all on this subject, to use these words. We must not be too fastidious, or thin-skinned, or particular on a point like that. While we are not in any degree to advertise our Christianity by our language, there are occasions, and this is one, when these things are necessary.

I want to say, in closing, that I hear almost extraordinary accounts of you Harvard men. Robert Browning once came to the Edinburgh students to talk to them; and he said, after he had gone away, that he had never in his life seen such a body of young men. Now I have no acquaintance with you whatever; but I have been asking up and down this district what sort of men the Harvard men are, and I want to let you know that you have a fairly good character. So far as I can learn, you have a character such as none of our Scotch universities have. Now live up to it. Let this university in the years to come be famous over America not only for its education, but for its sense of honor and manliness, and purity and Christianity. Seek first the kingdom of God. You know the whole truth. Live it. Want of interest in religion does not acquit you of taking your share in it. Why should I be here to talk to you? A Scotchman hates talking. I believe an American is dying to talk all the time. Well, I say want of religion does not absolve you from taking your share of it. The fact that you do not care about Christ does not alter the fact that Christ cares about you, that He wants you men, and that His kingdom cannot go on unless He gets such men as you. Are we to leave the greatest scheme that has ever been propounded to be carried out by duffers? It is easier, somebody says, to criticise the greatest scheme superbly than to do the smallest thing possible. The man who is looking on from the outside sees things in the game that the players do not see. He sees this bit of bad play and that. Well, stop criticising the game. Take off your coat, and come and help us. Our side is strong, and it is getting stronger; but we want the best men. Christianity ought to have the superlative men here in every department—in classics, in poetry, in literature, in humor, in everything that goes to the making of a man. The best gifts should be given to Christ. We are apt to despise Christianity and keep away from it because there are many weak-minded people in it. That is one reason why we ought to take off our coats and throw ourselves into it, heart and soul. And I leave you with that appeal. I appeal to the strong men here to consider their position and see if they can do anything better with their life than to help on this great cause.

An Address to the Man Who Is down

To-night I want to talk to the man who is down, to the man who has his back to the wall, and who is being embattled by his own temptations. It is, perhaps, not an academic subject, but it is the greatest of all subjects on which one can speak to young men. There are men here who are lost in the abyss; but there are more men who are on the brink of the precipice. Temptation is a universal experience—the one thing that makes every man his brother, and creates within any one who thinks about it a grave sense of tenderness as he thinks of those around him, when he remembers that every man he meets has the same black spot in his nature that he has, and the same terrible fight going on from day to day. But, gentlemen, temptation is more than a universal experience. It is an individual thing. Just as you have your own handwriting, your own face, or your own walk, you have your own temptation— different in every case, but generally some one temptation which means everything to you, which sums up the whole battle of life, and which, if you could conquer, you would conquer the world. That temptation follows you wherever you go like your shadow. I have gone into the heart of Africa. When I opened the curtains of my tent in the morning, the first face I saw was the hideous face of my own temptation. Go where you like, you cannot avoid that. It will follow you wherever you go, and lie with you in the grave. Temptation is not only a universal experience and a personal experience, but you have doubtless noticed this about it, that it is very lonely. It cuts a man off in a moment from all his fellowmen; and in the silence of his own heart he finds himself fighting out that battle on which the issues of life hang. Christ trod the wine press alone, and so do you and I. That is one of the things that makes it harder, because there is no one to blame us when we go wrong, and there is no one to applaud us when we do right.

More than that, temptation is a pitiless thing. It goes into the church and picks off the man in the pulpit. It goes into the university and picks off the flower of the class. It goes into the Senate and picks off the great man. Let him that thinketh he standeth, however high up, however sheltered, take heed lest he fall. Why is it that we have to run the gauntlet of temptation all our lives, and what does it mean? Can we analyze it? We have seen its strength. Can we find out whence it comes and how to meet it? There are many theories as to how it came into our nature. Some think there is a virus in human nature somewhere, a bias towards wrong; but I don't think we need to look very far for the origin at least of a great many of our temptations. We have in our bodies the residua of the animal creation. We have bones and muscles and organs which are now mere curiosities, but which once played a great part in the life of our progenitor; and I suppose it is now accepted as a scientific fact, at all events so far as the body is concerned, that it has come down the long ladder from the invertebrate world. That is to say, we have in our nature a part of the animal; and if we have an animal's body in us, we have to a certain extent the residua of an animal's mind, of an animal's proclivities and passions. Whether that is the origin of them or not, it is certain every man among us has a certain residuum of the animal in him. After passing through the animal stage, it is believed that man passed through a long, long discipline in the savage state; so that, in addition to the animal, relics of the savage are still left in our nature.

There are two great classes of sins—sins of the body and sins of the disposition. The prodigal son is a typical instance of sins of the body; and the elder brother a typical illustration of sins of the disposition. He was just as bad as the prodigal, probably worse. The one set of temptations comes from the animal and the other from the savage. What are the characteristics of the savage? Laziness for one thing, and selfishness for another. The savage does nothing but lie in the sun all day and allow the fruits to drop into his mouth. He has no struggle for life. Nature has been so kind as to supply all his wants; and he is, above all, characteristic of selfishness. He has no one to think about or care for, nor has he any capacity. A great preacher said not long ago to his congregation that he would tell them the mark of the beast, and that he also knew its number. He said the mark of the beast was selfishness, and its number was No. 1. Now the mark of the beast, selfishness, is in every man's breast, less or more. We are built in three stories—the bottom, the animal; a little higher up, the savage; and on the top, the man. That is the old Pauline trichotomy—body, soul, spirit. Paul spoke of this body of death. Science speaks of it in almost precisely the same language. Whatever the origin, that is the construction of a man. He is built in those three layers. With this analysis, it is perhaps easier to see how temptation may be met.

Many a man goes through life hanging his head with shame and living without his self-respect because he has never discovered the distinction between temptation and sin. It is only when a man sees temptation coming and goes out to meet it, welcomes it, plays with it and invites it to be his guest that it passes from temptation into sin; but, until he has opened the door of his own accord and let it in, he has done no wrong. He has been a tempted man—not a sinful man. The proof, of course, that temptation is no sin is that Christ was tempted in all points like as we are, yet without sin. Many a man is thrown back in his attempts to live a new life by the clinging to him of this residua of his past; and he does not discover until perhaps too late that there is nothing wrong in these things until they have passed a certain point. If he sees them coming and turns his back upon them, he has not sinned. Indeed, temptation is not only not sin, but it is the most valuable ingredient in human nature. Who was it that said, "The greatest of all temptations is to be without any"? The man who has no temptation has no chance of becoming a man at all. The only way to get character is to have temptation. If a man never exercises his muscle, he will get no muscle. If a man never exercises his moral nature in opposing temptation, he will get no muscle in his character. Temptation is an opportunity of virtue. What makes a good picture? Practice. What makes a good oarsman? Practice. What makes a good cricketer? Practice. Temptation is the practice of the soul; and the man who has most temptations has most practice. I fancy we all imagine we have more temptations than anybody else. That is a universal delusion. But, instead of praying to be delivered from our temptations, we ought to try to understand their essential place in the moral world. Taken from us, these would leave us without a chance of becoming strong men. We should be insipid characters, flaxen and useless. That is why the New Testament says the almost astonishing thing: "Count it all joy when ye fall into divers temptations." We are apt to call it hard lines because we are tempted. James says, count it joy; congratulate yourself because of your own temptation. It is the struggle for life almost solely which has helped on the evolution of the animal kingdom, passing on into the moral region and giving you practice in growth.

Now, then, granting that this discipline is to be ours, that every day of our lives we have to face temptation, how are we to set about it? We have seen that temptation lies in the projection on the human area of our life of the animal and of the savage. I think the first thing we have to do is to deal decisively with those two parts of our nature. The animal body was finished thousands and thousands of years ago. Nature took a long time to work it out, then stopped and went on to develop the mind. Let us recognize the development of the body as a fact in the past, and have no more to do with it. The body is finished. The hand of creation is done working at it. That is what Paul meant very largely when he gave it as his advice to men to get over temptation, "Reckon ye yourselves dead." Reckon that all beneath. It is not only wrong to allow the body to prevail in a man's life, but it is a denial of his development. It is unnatural and irrational. It is contrary to the teachings of science, borrowed altogether from the teachings of religion. Therefore, the first thing a man must do is to make up his mind that the body which is prompting him is a dead thing and is to be taken as a dead thing. If we can give our animal nature its true place, we will soon learn to rise above it. What did Cato do when he was buffeted? Ask Seneca. He did not strike back, fly into a passion: he did not resent it, but denied that it had been done. That is to say, the body being nothing, nothing had happened.

But that is not enough. We cannot live negatively. It is not enough to forsake the old life, the old habit; but we must take another piece of advice which I think the New Testament also sums up for us in language of exceeding simplicity and yet of absolute scientific accuracy. Paul says: "Walk in the spirit." Live in the top flat. You find yourself living in the animal part of your being. Escape and get into the upper story, where the roof is open to God, and whre you can move amongst beautiful things, and amongst holy memories and amongst high ideals. Walk in the spirit and ye shall not fulfill the lusts of the flesh. A man can't do it. That is to say, he has to evolve the past, the animal and the savage, and develop the new nature. The new nature is renewed from day to day, little by little. Just as the body is built up, microscopic cell by microscopic cell, so the new nature is built up by a long series of crucifixions of the old nature, by taking in food from the higher world and getting those things built into our nature which work for righteousness and truth and beauty and purity.

Now, the man who encourages the higher part of his nature continuously will get an absolute victory over the lower parts of his being. He will come to live in those higher parts of his being. It will become as habitual to live there as it was to live in the lower; and, while this building up is going on within, there will be the degeneration of the old nature. How has man evolved past the animal and the savage, and how has so much that is in them passed away from him? By mere disuse. And so, by the mere disuse of the propensities of the body and the discouragement of selfish and petty interests, by merely giving up the animal ways and the animal passions, and the savage tempers and the savage laziness, the impulse, the function which makes these things, will wither—atrophy. As the one goes on, the other inevitably follows. As the old man passes away, the new man is renewed in righteousness. That can be explained not only in the language of development but in the language of psychology as a perfectly rational principle. A man cannot have two things in consciousness at the same moment. Suppose a man has been lost out in the West and wandered away from the railway depot where he had put up at a hotel. Perhaps he has been four or five days on the prairie. One day he staggers back, almost dropping with hunger and calls out for food; but finds lying upon his table, while waiting for food, a telegram reporting the sudden death of his wife. The hunger is gone, completely gone. The man who was perishing a few moments ago is now absolutely above it; and if I could keep up the emotion of sorrow, I could keep down forever the appetite of hunger. If you want to get over an appetite on philosophical principles, not to speak of religion, the thing to do is to pass into another region, and let your mind be preoccupied with something higher. Unless you take in the higher, it is tremendously difficult to crush out the lower. The new man can only be put on as the old man is put off.

You remember Augustine's history of temptation in four words—cogitatio, imaginatio, delectatio and assensio: a thought, a picture, a fascination, and a fall. You can cut off the series between the first and second. Between the second and third, it is almost impossible. Between the third and fourth, it is absolutely impossible. When the image is thrown upon the screen and you are delighting in it and it is just beginning to enthrall you, you can still do one thing. You can suddenly throw another image on the screen and look at that. If you look for two seconds at the first image you are lost; but if you look one second you are not yet lost, and there is still a chance to be saved. You can throw another image over it and let the first dissolve away; and, by the mere possession of consciousness, you have got over that temptation.

You see, then, how, upon merely natural principles, it is possible to fight temptation. If we simply walk in the spirit, we shall not fulfill the lusts of the flesh. We must evolve past them, in plain words. By cultivating ideals of all kinds and by strengthening our moral nature by all the opportunities we can get in society, in literature and in the church, we will gradually accumulate a body, a higher body, of life and mind and truth, in which we can live; and the old tenements in which we lived will not only be uninhabited but uninhabitable. Hence the value of everything that is beautiful and pure and lovely and wholesome in the world; and not only their use as auxiliaries to the religious life, but as indispensable to it; because all these are things in the higher nature, and the man who cultivates them is building up a region in which he can live. A man must live. He must live in the body, in the savage or in the man. At every moment he must live, and so at every moment he must make his choice. He cannot suppress it. If you take this subject in terms of energy, you will find that the energy which leads to sin must not be suppressed, but must be transformed into an energy which leads to virtue; so that when the desire to do something wrong comes in, instead of trying to suppress that desire, we have simply to turn the helm in the right direction; and in the new channel it will not only save us from a fall which we would have had, if we had allowed it to go the other way, but it will carry us higher towards the new life.

Now I have tried to explain the way in which any man here can rise above himself and be a man. I care not how far he has dropped. It is an historical fact that a man can be saved to the uttermost. You say to me, is there no religion in all this? It is all religion. You say, do I not need to put more religion into it? The more the better. I have spoken of walking in the spirit. I have spoken of ideals. I know no ideal that will act so promptly as the ideal of the perfect Man. I know no picture that you can throw upon the screen which will fascinate more immediately than the picture of the character of Christ. You may throw people upon the screen, a line of poetry, an epigram from a moralist, a memory of your mother, a warning of some one you love, and all these are reflections in some form of Christ; and they will all be effective up to a point. But most of all effective is the power of Christ Himself; and, unless a man has a moral environment which is full of these things, he cannot live. There is no hope for his new life, unless he has that. No man can live without these things morally. Take that gas which gives us light. The light is not in the gas. It is half in the air and half in the gas. Take away the half from the air, and the gas goes out. "Without me, ye can do nothing." Your life will go out. Without Me, whether as the Light of the world itself, or as diffused through books, and through men and through churches, without that your life will come to nothing; but, if you take that and all the reflections of it, and let these constitute a spiritual atmosphere about you, your redemption from this hour is a certainty. There is no haphazard about

Christianity. It is based upon the laws of nature and the laws of the human mind.

The man who lives in Christ cannot go wrong. He will be kept. In the nature of things, he must be kept. He cannot sin. You remember John said: "Whosoever sinneth hath not seen Him, neither known Him." John's Friend was such, so inspiring and so influential, that it was inconceivable to John that anybody could ever have met Him without forevermore trying to live like Him. Sin is abashed in the presence of the purity of Jesus Christ. There are many heroes in life. They will all help a man; but we will get on better and quicker by giving ourselves to Christ.

I have just two things to add. The first is: if any man here to-night takes this seriously and means business; if he means for the future not to keep up the sham fight that he has been pretending to wage, and means to get to the bottom of things, let me ask him for a few days from this time to treat himself as a man who has been very ill and dare not do anything. Let him consider himself as a convalescent for a few weeks and take care where he goes, what he reads, what he looks at, and the people he speaks to. He is not strong enough for the outer air. When he first begins the new life, he is young and tender. Therefore, let him beware of the first few days. Mortality is greatest amongst children for the first few hours: then it is greater for the first few days; then it is great for the next few months, and lessens as the children grow older. If you are careful not to catch cold for the first few weeks after you begin to lead a new life, you will succeed; but, if you do to-morrow what you did to-day, you will go wrong, because you are not strong enough to resist. You will have to build up this new body cell by cell, day by day, just as the old body of temptation has been built up. If any man here knows any other man who is in that convalescent condition, let him take care, and neither by jest, or word, or temptation, throw that man back. Stand by him, if you know such a man. If you are such a man, do not be ashamed to get somebody else to back you and go along with you. Very few men can live a solitary Christian life. You will find it a great source of strength to get another man's life wound about you. You can help each other.

The other thing I want to say is this: Do not imagine that you can get deliverance from sin alone—I mean without getting other things, and without doing other things. Deliverance from sin is only a part of the Christian life—by no means the whole. It is only one wing of the new nature; but no man can get on with one wing. Deliverance from temptation is only one function of the new nature. Therefore, you must consecrate your whole life to Christianity, and go into it wholly and with a whole heart, if you expect to get deliverance in this one direction; and the best way you can do that is to make up your mind that you will give much of your life to Christianity, to purify the air of the world, so that other men will feel less temptation than you do. Sin is a kind of bacillus, and it cannot take root in the world unless there is a soil, and it is our business to make the world's soil pure and sanitarily sweet, so that the disease of sin cannot exist.

One Way to Help Boys

I am very much pleased to find the Boys' Brigade receiving University recognition. I am not aware that it has had this honor before in its history.

The idea of the Brigade is this. It is a new movement for turning out boys, instead of savages. The average boy, as you know, is a pure animal. He is not evolved; and, unless he is taken in hand by somebody who cares for him and who understands him, he will be very apt to make a mess of his life—not to speak of the lives of other people. We endeavor to get hold of this animal. You do not have the article here, and do not quite understand the boy I mean. The large cities of the old world are infested by hundreds and thousands of these ragamuffins, as we call them—young roughs who have nobody to look after them. The Sunday-school cannot handle these boys. The old method was for somebody to form them into a class and try to get even attention from them. Half the time was spent in securing order.

The new method is simply this: You get a dozen boys together, and, instead of forming them into a class, you get them into some little hall and put upon every boy's head a little military cap that costs in our country something like twenty cents, and you put around his waist a belt that costs about the same sum, and you call him a soldier. You tell him, "Now, Private Hopkins, stand up. Hold up your head. Put your feet together." And you can order that boy about till he is black in the face, just because he has a cap on his head and a belt around his waist. The week before you could do nothing with him. If he likes it, you are coming next Thursday night. He is not doing any favor by coming. You are doing him a favor; and if he does not turn up at eight o'clock, to the second, the door will be locked. If his hair is not brushed and his face washed, he cannot enter. Military discipline is established from the first moment. You give the boys three-fourths of an hour's drill again, and in a short time you have introduced quite a number of virtues into that boy's character. You have taught him instant obedience. If he is not obedient, you put him into the guard house, or tell him he will be drummed out of the regiment; and he will never again disobey. If he is punctual and does his drill thoroughly, tell him that at the end of the year he will get a stripe. He will get a cent's worth of braid. You have his obedience, punctuality, intelligence and attention for a year for one cent. Then you have taught him courtesy. He salutes you and feels a head taller. Everything is done as if you were a real captain and he a real private. He calls you "Captain." Each boy has a rifle that costs a dollar; but there is no firing. There is a bayonet drill without a bayonet. The first year they have military drill, and the second year bayonet exercises—an absolute copy of the army drill. The Brigade inculcates a martial, but not a warlike, spirit. The only inducement to bring the boys together at first is the drill. You might think it is a very poor one; but it is about the strongest inducement you could offer.

That is the outward machinery; but it is a mere take-in. The boy doesn't know it. The real object of the Brigade is to win that boy for Christianity—to put it quite plainly. It does not make the slightest secret of its aims.

On all its literature is: "The object of the Brigade shall be the advancement of Christ's Kingdom among boys, and the promotion of habits of reverence, discipline, self-respect, and all that tends toward a true Christian manhood."

After you have your boy and are sure of him, every drill is opened with a couple of minutes of prayer. The boys stand in line at "attention," with caps off, while a sort of blessing is asked. Then drill for three-fourths of an hour. After that the Captain gives them a little talk about anything—business prosperity, courtesy, courage, temptation, or anything. After that, all repeat the Lord's Prayer and dismiss. Then on Sunday almost all the companies have Bible class, with the same punctuality, interest and attention as during the week day. The boy treats his Captain as before. They sit like statues during the Bible lesson; and, if they are not there to the minute, they are shut out. Having influence over them, the Captain maintains it, and how much more apt the boys will be to pick up what he says. The thorough-going Captain will of course do a great deal more than in the Bible class; and very few stop at that. Some men get up football clubs and get fields, give up their own Saturday afternoons —which are a great holiday with us—to act as umpire for the boys' matches. Our captains are just one remove from the boys whom they teach, so that the boys are not at all afraid of them. The presence of the captain on the athletic field means, in the first place, that there will be no foul language and no foul play. And he, of course, thus increases his influence over them tenfold. Then in many cases they start a boys' club where they have a room open every night, where they have debates, newspapers and books. Then the captain gets to know the boys personally. He has them up to tea now and then, and gets to know their people.

In addition to that general work, there are one or two additions which are thrown in by special companies according to their own inclination. A great many have started military bands. Ambulance classes are becoming exceedingly popular. After drilling two or three winters the work gets flat; so they invent new things. Boys cannot join this Brigade until they are twelve years of age, and cannot clear out until they are seventeen. The boys hate to clear out; and the fact that they will have to leave induces them to make better use of their time. Of course they are not turned adrift. The captain sees that they get into good hands. Then every year, in a city of the size of Boston, for instance, all the boys belonging to the Brigade would be gathered together for a church service. If too many for one church, two would be secured, and the boys would assemble and march to the service and get a boys' sermon. At Christmas, every boy in the Brigade gets from his officer a little two-cent book. And there are a number of other little things that link the captain and the boys together and the different companies together.

This organization was started within a mile of where I live in Glasgow in 1883, by a Mr. Smith, who was a soldier, and who was not making much of a Sunday-school class he taught, and who conceived the idea of giving them military discipline. In our country we have grown to such an extent that already there are, I think, 22,000 boys belonging to the Brigade, and I think between 1,100 and 1,200 officers—captains and lieutenants. This Brigade has been worth starting for the sake of the officers alone.

Perhaps one thousand of these officers would have belonged to the unemployed rich and educated, if they had not struck this particular line of work. There are multitudes of young men who do not go to prayer meeting or see their way to teach in Sunday-school. Many are extremely fastidious as to what particular work they will do, and many are not cut out for these recognized fields. But here is a work that does not make any particular strain on any part of his nature. He simply gives himself and his muscular Christianity. So we think this has been worth pushing for the sake of the officers alone. We know a great many men have been made for life simply by a year or two of contact with these boys. If they develop the boys, the boys develop them.

Now, you have this movement started in America. I find the most crass ignorance on this subject here; but in some respects you are ahead of us. One of the first things you do with the boys is to start a newspaper. The conflagration has broken out in a somewhat remarkable way in California, and they must have a great many companies. As usual, when you take up anything in this country from anywhere else, you improve upon it or carry it to development in other directions.

Now, you do some things here we do not do, and of which I am not perfectly sure we would wholly approve. They strike us as being slightly against some of the fundamental principles for which we work. For instance, I notice that the boys here have a uniform, and that the officers have a uniform. We can make a boy for about fifty cents, not including the brass in his face; but here in America the uniform costs as follows:

(See Boys' Brigade Manual, U. S. of A.)
Fatigue blouses (I suppose they have paid duty on these blouses) $3.35
Pants 3.35
Fatigue caps, first quality 0.75
Belts 0.75
Plain bugles 0.25
Signal service 1.20
U. S. Army bunting flags 9.50

Silk cord for same 3.50
Bugler's stripes for pants 1.50
Extra fine officers' fatigue blouses 6.75
Pants with stripes 6.50
U. S. Army officers' overcoats with hoods $27 to 32.00

Well, you see that means business at any rate. But what we dislike about it is that it emphasizes the military side too much. We have refused to admit any company into the Brigade that wears a uniform. There are one or two in the country, but we don't have them. We don't want the boys to feel soldiers beyond the point that we need them to feel soldiers. We don't want them to thirst for blood and come over here and fight you or anybody else. We simply want to get them disciplined. I suppose there must be in this country quite a number of companies equipped at very considerable expense. These boys cannot afford to buy these uniforms for themselves, and they are very frequently bought by subscription.

This organization in America is almost always organized within the church. In the old country every organization must be associated, not necessarily with the church, but with some stable body that will be back of it and be a sponsor for it. It is usually the church—sometimes the Y. M. C. A. In this country the initiatory is frequently taken by the minister. I find the ministers here preserve the dew of their youth and the freshness of their manhood, and they are not at all the starchy kind of people one meets in some other countries. It is not because they are not fit for this, but the ministers must not have all the plums. They have enough to do. Here and there we have some keen ministers at this work, but, as a rule, we try to keep it among the laity.

In this country you make the boys promise that as long as they are members of the Boys' Brigade they will not use liquor and tobacco, will obey the rules and set an example of good conduct. The question is whether pledges are right fair to a boy at all. I very much question whether it is wise to put a strong pledge like that upon anybody. We exact no pledge whatever. It seems to me to be the difference between compulsory chapel attendance and optional, as it is here, to make a boy not smoke by compulsion. If he can be made moral by the influences that are brought to bear upon him, it is more apt to last.

Now I suppose I was asked to present this subject to you in behalf of enlisting one or two of you in the service. I do not know myself of any bit of work to which I would rather give what spare time I have than this. The boy is open to receive impressions in a way that is marked. It is possible to get hold of him. There are thousands of these boys who have been turned outside in. I have watched them. I remember the annual inspection of one of the first companies. When the prizes were given, it was my duty to pin the medals on the two leading boys' breasts. When the first boy came up, there was scarcely a place on his coat strong enough to bear the pin. His coat was one mass of patches that could scarcely hold together. He was clean. The next year I noticed he had on a much better coat, and I am sure he is now on his way to turn out to be a good man. I do not know anything that would pay any of you better than this. It lies near a young man's nature to take up such work. I do not think there is anything easier than to win a boy. You get him wound about you, and he lives through your spectacles and tries to please you. Adapt it any way you please; but I should like very much if after to-night some of you would write for some of this literature and take the trouble to spread it.

We gave the boys books each Christmas. Two years ago I wrote a book and offered fifty-three prizes. The boys competing were to write a letter addressed to "My Dear Baxter," and answer the question, "What are a Boy's Temptations, and How is He to Meet Them?" Well, I got about 450 dissections of the boys in answer to that offer. One of the thirty prizes went to California. I never saw such a revelation of the interior of a boy as I saw after reading those letters. Every boy, almost, out of the lot, pleaded guilty to four sins. Every boy, apparently, is a liar and a thief. These were the first two things that they all confessed. The third confession was that they all swore; and the fourth great temptation or sin to a boy was smoking—which is not a sin at all. It showed me that the boys were very badly taught, and that they have no definite conception of sin.

Every one of these Brigades, almost without an exception, is connected with the church. The Bible class is held in the church; and the drill is usually there, too. It is thoroughly under the wing of the church. The movement is so religious that there is never any religious opposition to it, and it is entirely undenominational.

An Appeal to the Outsider; or the Claims of Christianity

I am asked to talk specially to what we call in Scotland "the outsider"—the man who has not seen his way to throw in his lot with Christian men. We have made a specialty of the outsider in our university work in the old country. We have laid all our plans to interest him. He is generally the best man in the university; and for some years we have arranged all our Christian work and worship with a view to that type of man. We have laid down one or two principles. The first one is that none of us in any shape or form shall encourage cant. By that I mean sanctimoniousness, anything that is falsetto, any unreal expression of emotion or exaggeration of feeling. A second principle we have had to lay down is that no religious man shall interfere in any shape or form with the university amusements. Time after time I have seen at our religious meetings twelve out of the fifteen university football team; and we have always had amongst our foremost men the best athletes in the university. We have also laid it down as a principle that we shall not interfere with any university work. We have tried to get hold of the busiest men and interest them in whatever is going on, believing that a man may do his university work thoroughly and yet do something in the way of helping on the Christian life of his fellow students. In the Medical Faculty, where we have from 1,800 to 2,000 students, and which is our largest faculty in Edinburgh University, at the end of the four years' course we have the "Blue Ribbon Medical Course" scholarship. It is given to the man who has stood first all along the line for four years. Now the man who for the last four years has taken this scholarship has been not only one of the most active workers in the Christian community, but actually the secretary of the movement. I do not mean that one man has done that for four years; but the last four men have been not only the leading men in the scientific and professional studies, but the leading men in the Christian life of the place. With such a record as that you can understand that Christianity is, at all events, respected.

We never have any religious meetings on week days. We do not want the professors to say we are taking up the time the men ought to give other things. We believe a man's business at a college, and his religion, too, is to do his work. The meetings we have had, therefore, were on Sundays.

Another rule that we have had to make is never to interfere with a man's views. We want a man's life. We do not want his opinion. We do not start a man with a creed. We believe that the man arrives at a creed; and we take into our ranks any man who has any desire to seek the Kingdom of God. That, of course, had widened the door to a very large number of men who would have kept out, if we had been exclusive. But while we do not underrate a creed, while we believe that theological doctrines are just as scientific doctrines; yet religion is an art, and we can get men to practice the art who will arrive, we hope, in their future life, at something of the scientific principles which underlie it; but we make it a barrier to no man at the start that he knows little. In fact, a man enters the school of Christ as he enters a university. That is to say, he enters, not as a professor, but as a student. He comes to learn; and we believe the best way to learn is to let the man matriculate and begin.

If you ask me what obstacles we find specially in the way, I think the chief obstacle we meet is the revolt in thinking men's minds against popular and spurious and weak forms of Christianity. Men come to the institution who have been very strictly brought up, and they are not able, after a few months' college discipline, to believe the things they used to believe. A gentleman in Boston said to me a few days ago that he had a son at Harvard and that the young man had the audacity to come to him not long ago and tell him that he didn't believe so and so. I said to him: "Sir, what a splendid fellow your son must be." He preferred truth to comfort. A man is to be encouraged to think about religious matters. If Christianity cannot bear thinking about, it is not worth going in for.

One other thing that one finds is the idea many men have that it is a dull thing to go in for Christianity. Now, of course, that is simply not true. It is not true in fact, and it is not true in theory. It has, doubtless, more concern for a man's temperament and body than his creed; but if there is anything that can put sunniness or brightness into a man's life, it is Christianity. Christianity professes to cure dullness. Some of the greatest words in the Bible are "joy," "rest," "comfort." Christianity cures depression and gloom by removing the causes of it. What makes men depressed? Self-concentration, as a rule. When a man is wrapped up in himself, seeking only his own, he finds he is seeking a very shallow object, and very soon gets to the end of it; hence all the springs of life have nothing to act upon, and depression follows. Now, Christianity cures that by trying to take a man out of himself, and by showing him that his true life is in living out of himself.

Another source of dullness is the thwarting of the ambitions that we have. We get down in spirits because we do not get the recognition we think we deserve, because we are snubbed and slighted, because we are not at the top. Christianity cures that by a single sentence. It says: "The meek shall inherit the earth." There is no connection between Christianity and a dull life. It is the want of Christianity that makes any life dull. Christianity offers a young man, or an old man, or any man, a more abundant life than the life he is living—more life as life goes, more happiness in life, more intensity in life, more worthiness in life.

That, however, is perhaps not so great an obstacle, comparatively a trifling one, as the thought many men have that it is an unscientific thing in these days to endorse Christianity. Now it may be unscientific to endorse some forms in which Christianity is presented, but Christianity itself is a thoroughly scientific thing. There is nothing the least narrow about anything that Christ ever said. On the contrary, Christ said the broadest things that have ever been said; and he never rebuked breadth, but constantly rebuked narrowness. In His day there were three great philosophical, theological schools. There were the Pharisees, who were so narrow that they could not see spirit for form. There were the Sadducees, who were so narrow that they could not see spirit for matter. And there were the Essenes, who could not see matter for spirit. Christ was always rebuking these sects simply on account of their narrowness. His own view of life was as broad as the heavens. He took in every man and every part of every man. His religion was not kept back by any geographical or ethnographical limits. It was the religion of humanity.

You say, "But it is well known that many scientific men are opposed to Christianity." I ask you to give me their names. If you run over the names of the large figures in science at this moment, you will find that the majority are not only in favor of Christianity, but have expressed themselves in favor of it.

Mr. Huxley has never said anything against Christianity. He has defined the position of science. He says, "Science is not Christianity, nor is it anti-Christianity. It is extra-Christianity." He has thrown an arrow, with a little poison on it, perhaps, at some of the outworks of Christianity; but he has never said one word against Christ or the words or spirit of Christ. And it matters little what a man does to the outworks so long as he respects and is compelled to respect Christ; and Christianity is always respected, however humbly it is lived, by the wisest men.

The other day I came upon a statement by a Fellow of the Royal Society with regard to this subject, a sentence of which I should like to read to you. The Royal Society of London, as you know, is probably one of the first scientific bodies in the world. This man says: "I have known the British Association for the Advancement of Science under forty-one different presidents—all leading men of science. On looking over these forty-one names, I count twenty, who, judged by their public utterances or private communications, are men of Christian belief and character; while, judged by the same test, only four disbelieve in direct divine revelation."

You point to Mr. Darwin. Mr. Darwin never had, and never gave himself, a chance. He was brought up on Paley's Natural Theology—a great book in its day, but a book which Darwin himself made it impossible to read to-day; and he was bombarded with that book, and with religion along that line; and we have no evidence that he ever studied Christianity in any other form. But wherever he saw it, he respected it. When he was on the Island of Terra del Fuego, he saw the lowest subjects in the world. He told the missionaries they might go home. It was an impossibility, from the point of view of science, that these men could ever be elevated. A very few years after, Mr. Darwin wrote a letter to the secretary of that missionary society saying that he had found out what a great change had come over these islands—a certain amount of civilization had been introduced, and morality had been established; and he would like to withdraw what he had said. He enclosed a check for twenty five dollars for the work of the society; and he continued sending in his annual contribution to the end of his life.

Perhaps the greatest name known to you in the old country is that of Sir William Thompson, now Lord Kelvin, Professor of Physics in Glasgow University. If you go into his class room any day you like, you will hear him open his lecture with prayer.

It is not true that the scientific men have given up Christianity. Many of them have given up imitations of Christianity, spurious forms of it; but the thing itself stands untouched.

You ask me, "What, then, do you retain? Do you dilute Christianity until it means little or nothing—so little that anybody can call himself a Christian?" On the contrary, we make it the most severe thing, the most definite thing, that a man could choose for his object in life. We make it a necessity that a man shall be turning, that he shall seek first the Kingdom of God. He may choose his own way of doing it; but he must put that before him as an ambition and as his career to seek first the Kingdom of God. We say nothing to those men about saving their souls. We say to them: "Gentlemen, save your lives. Do something with your life. Let that energy, that talent, go out to some purpose. The world needs the knowledge you have, the impulses you can give; aye, and the criticisms that you can offer upon the religious forms round about. It needs all these things. Save your lives. Do something with them." The Kingdom of God, according to Christ's own definition, is leaven; it is salt; it is light. Can you tell me what is going to raise this country, for instance, if it is not to be Christianity? If you take the Christianity out of Boston, weak as some of it may be, and inconsistent as some of it may be, in fifty years it will be uninhabitable by a respectable man or woman. Was it Mr. Lowell who said: "Show me ten square miles in any part of the world, outside of Christianity, where the life of man and the purity of woman are safe, and I will give up Christianity"? There are no such ten square miles in any part of the world. Many things can lift society a little; but, as a matter of fact and history, the thing that has lifted the nations of the world to their present level has been, in some form or other, direct or diffused, the Christianity of Christ. Christian men are to be not only the leaven of the world, but they are to be the salt of the earth. The world is not only sunken, needing to be raised, but it is rotten, and needing to be purified. Salt is that which saves from corruption. Christianity is the salt of the earth. It is the great antiseptic of society. Christian men are the light of the world. The light of Christ was the light of men; and other men are to catch that light and radiate it upon the world.

You point me to other teachers, many of them very great, many of them with great messages for the world—Socrates, Plato—a long list of names;

but, allowing all their goodness, can one of them be put beside Christ as a mere teacher? Socrates went about the world asking questions. Christ went about the world answering questions. That was the difference. Socrates was looking for truth. Christ said truth is in living. I am the truth; and the man who lives like Me will live true, and all the wrong in the mind will be corrected. You cannot help seeing truth.

Now, gentlemen, what do you think of that for a life, for a career? You do not know what to do with yourself. What do you think of being a crystal of salt in a community such as this city, or a little cell of leaven which cannot help, by the mere contagion of its presence, passing on influence and life to things round about it, or being a light to the dark people, perhaps the dark Christians, if you like, round about, too?

Do the workingmen of this country not need light? What is to alter the critical condition of the working classes in this country, if it is not to be the teaching of Christianity in some form? What is to guide these labor movements and to work upon the minds in all directions, to make this country continuously prosperous? Men who have looked deepest into these problems have either given them up or seen only one solution, and that is in the teaching of Christ and the application of His principles to common life. These principles are not in the air. They are justified by every fact and law of nature.

I believe in Christianity, first of all, not because I believe in this book. I believe in this book because I believe in Christianity. Religion does not come out of the Bible. The Bible comes out of religion. I believe in Christianity because I believe in evolution. Christianity is to me further evolution. I know no better definition of it than that. The forces of nature carry a man up to a certain point and there they stop. Then the psychic forces carry him up another point to the evolution of mind. Then the moral forces come in and carry him up a little further. Then the vis a tergo, the struggle for life that pushes him on, is reinforced by a vis a fronto; and he sees ideals before him, and is drawn up higher and higher, from strength to strength, until he reaches the fullness of the stature of the perfect man. That is pure evolution, the evolution of the man toward the ideal, toward the perfect man Jesus Christ. This principle of which I have been speaking, of a man giving his life to other people, to help on his country, is in the very, heart of nature. There are two great principles in nature by which all things work and by which all things are moved. The one is the struggle for life. Every plant and animal starts out to nourish itself. That struggle goes on along the line of the function of nutrition. There is the struggle for the life of others—the function of reproduction. These two functions make up life. Now, most of us live along the line of the first. All our lives, nearly, are centered in that; but that is only one half of the life appointed by nature. There is the struggle for the life of others, the function of reproduction, and in its higher forms everything that is high lies. All the happiness in life, in reality, has come along the second of these two lines, and not along the first. All the life of the world, in reality, lies on the side of reproduction. A plant takes a little bit of itself and gives it away. It lives by death. It dies; the life goes on. This chapel is built upon death. That book is death. Those pillars are the death of men. Those clothes are the death of animals. Every part of life and everything in life is kept alive by death. The animal gives off a part of itself and dies. Its life goes on—has passed on; and I say all the comfort and happiness and beauty and luxury of life come along that line. Three-fourths of the world at this moment live upon rice. What is rice? It is a seed —a fruit, therefore, of reproduction. The world lives upon this altruistic principle. All the fruits of the world are the gifts of reproduction. All the drinks of the world are the fruits of reproduction —the milk of the cow, the sprouting grain, the malted liquor, the withered hop, the fruit of the vine, wine itself. All the beauty of the world comes along the line of reproduction—the feathers of the bird, the fire of the glow-worm, the face of a woman. All the music of the world is love music—the chorus of the insect, the song of the nightingale, the serenade of the lover. We live by what the function of reproduction has done for us; and the man who gives his life for what is going on in that line is living for the highest end in nature.

The struggle for life is waning every century, and by and by it will give place entirely to this other. Therefore, when Christ said, "Seek first the Kingdom of God," he propounded a perfectly scientific doctrine. He was offering man a life which would include all other lives, to which all other things would be heir.

Let me give you an illustration of what I mean. You are here at the university. You can't yet begin to do anything for your country, as you might. What you can do now is to leaven this university. What you can do is to get hold of some one man, whose life is of no account, and which is apparently not going to be of any account, and save that man, not for his own sake only, but because that is a piece of energy which has gone off but can be brought in and reclaimed and utilized for the good of man.

There was a medical student in Edinburgh University in his second year (our course is four years), who saw that he had been living there eighteen months entirely for himself. He had never done a hand's turn to be of any good or use to any one, and it hurt him. One day he determined that he would do something to help another man, and he remembered another undergraduate, who had come from the same country town as himself, and who had gone to pieces. He hunted him up. He found him half drunk in a very poor and shabby lodging. He told him that he would like him to come and live in his rooms; that he had nice rooms, and it was snugger than where he was. The other man stated he was in debt and could not leave. No. 1 went out of the room, paid the man's bill, sent for a carriage, bundled up his friend's things—and a newspaper held them all—and took him off to his own lodgings. The next morning he said: "Now, you and I are going to live together. Let us make a contract and both sign it."

There were four articles in it.

"First, neither one of us is to go out alone, unless absolutely necessary.

"Second, twenty minutes to be allowed to go from room to college for recitations. Overtime to be accounted for.

"Third, one hour to be given every night to recreation.

"Fourth, bygones to be bygones."

They both signed it. Everything went on well. They had lived together for six weeks when one night No. 2 sprang up, shut his book with a bang and said: "I can't stand this slow life. I must have a bust." "Very well," said No. 1, "you shall bust here. What do you want?" "I want some drink." "Well, you shall have it," said No. 1, and he got him something to drink and brought it to the room. No. 2 took it. Do you say it was a risk? His thirst was allayed and the wild beast was calmed. He settled down to his books for six weeks again, when the wild beast once more asserted itself. No. 1 gave it a meal to satisfy it, as before. No. 2 worked faithfully this time for three months before another outbreak. And so the thing went on. A year afterward No. 2 said to No. 1: "You never tell me what you are reading at the recreation hour. I think I see you read the Bible sometimes. You never talked to me on that subject." Talked to him about it! What was the use of talking to a man about Christianity when he was living it every hour of his life? He had done his work without ever having said a word. No. 2 was dying to learn his secret. I need not detail the rest. These two men passed out of the University at the end of their course. No. 1 passed a fairly good examination. No. 2, the man who was lost, graduated with honors and took the medal for his thesis. The last time I heard of No. 1 he was filling an important appointment in London, and No. 2 is known as "the Christian Doctor" of a village in Wales. Now that seems to me to be a thing worth living for; something to look back upon after one's college life is over.

No one knew anything about this. No. 1 was never known as a specially religious man, and yet, in his quiet way, he was living Christ in every direction; and he left more fragrance behind him when he was gone than a dozen of the noisier men.

I ask you, gentlemen, to save your lives, to save your college days, and I appeal to the generous side of you and ask you to remember your fellow men. Remember the man who is going to pieces; remember the man who is down, the man who is tempted. Perhaps if you would stand by him you could help him through. You need not make any great profession of religion. But, if you do that, you will make a great practice of it. It will amount to little, after the college course is over, that you have merely done your work and passed. What is the use of your passing, what is the use of your getting any degree, unless it is going to be of some use to somebody else? There is no particular reason why nine-tenths of us should be alive at all; but the man who begins to live for the Kingdom of God, who sees a chance to do a good turn here and a little one there, and shed a little light here and a little sunniness there, has something to live for. That man's life will never be lost. He lives a more abundant life. There is no other joy or light in the world except that.

And if you gentlemen are going to seek the Kingdom of God, I want to ask you to seek it first. Do not touch it unless you promise to seek it first. I promise you a miserable life and influence and a poor, broken, lost career, if you seek it second. Seek it first, or let it alone. Do not be an amphibian; no man can serve two masters, and, if you only knew it, it is a thousand times easier to seek first the Kingdom of God than to seek it second. I have not the slightest doubt there are many men who are seeking second the Kingdom of God, and their religion is a nuisance to them. It is hard to keep up, and they would get rid of it if they could. The cure is to seek it first, to make it the helm of life. Then only can a man's life go straight, and then only can he fulfill the destiny for which God has put him into the world.

Life on the Top Floor

You have had a great time on the mountains, but remember the mountain is not a place to live on. The Mount of Transfiguration is an episode, coming to a man from time to time; but it is not in the ordinary course of nature that a man should always live on the top of the mountain. The mountain is of use to send streams into the valley of our ordinary life, to fertilize and nourish what is there. Perhaps it is not possible that we shall all be living at the same pitch at which you have lived during the days of this week. Before the sacramental wine was dry on the lips of Peter he was untrue to his Saviour. A breakdown to the moral life is just as natural, and just as much a matter of law as the breakdown of an engine. It is important to get to the bottom of these causes. One of the most important things for us to study is the anatomy of the soul, the anatomy of temptation, and the physiology of sin.

You will not agree with me, perhaps, but I have a strong suspicion that the evolutionists are on the right track when they tell us that man's body has come up through the animal creation. Bone for bone, muscle for muscle and nerve for nerve, you and I are exactly the same as the higher vertebrae of the animal kingdom; and after we passed through the animal kingdom, it is supposed by the theorists, we underwent a long probation in which we were somewhat in the condition of the red Indian; and, just as we had the bodies of animals, we had to some extent the minds of animals and the dispositions of savages. If the animal has left me as its legacy a vertebral column and certain nerves, why should it not leave me a legacy of its modes and passions? And if I have once had as my ancestors a long race of savages, why should not the modes and predilections of the savage nature be still in my blood? If I have the blood of the tiger, shall I not have to some extent the spirit of a tiger? If I have the blood of a shark, shall I not be inclined sometimes to play the shark? If I have the blood of a fox, shall I not be inclined sometimes to be foxy? Well, it doesn't matter in the least whether that is true or not, but I appeal to you if it is not a fact that you find in yourselves the residuum of many animals and the disposition of many savages. If there is a man who has nothing of the animal in him, I should like you to introduce me to him. It doesn't matter where it came from. It is there, as a matter of fact. That is to say, man is built in three stories. He is a three-storied structure. On the ground floor there dwells the animal. Above that, on the second story, there is the savage. And on the third floor there is the man. Now, my brother, when you go wrong, it is not you who goes wrong, it is the man who lives in the bottom story. And when you collapse, when you imagine that it is impossible for you to recover again, remember that the true man in you is still there; and that although temptations may come to you from these lower parts of your nature, it is not essential that you should live in idle acquiescence to them. By taking to pieces the moral nature, one sees very clearly what temptation really is. It is the appeal of the animal to the man; and it is no sin for man to hear that appeal. It is no sin for a man to be tempted. In virtue of his nature, man must be tempted. It is when a man leaves the top story and deliberately walks down and spends an hour in the cellar that temptation passes from temptation into sin.

In the same way, one sees very clearly from that little piece of anatomy, how it is possible to overcome temptation. The remedy, of course, is simply to decline ever to move in the lower regions of one's being at all, to regard that as a thing evolved past, and to live constantly in the higher regions. When a man does that, it is impossible for him to break down. Put it in this way. An image is thrown upon the screen of your mind and you look at it. How can you dismiss it? You can only dismiss it by throwing another image on the screen which will be more beautiful, more pure and more attractive, and which, above all, will pre-occupy your mind so that the other image will fade away. It is impossible, I think, in most cases, for the man to deliberately fight the temptation when it comes in certain forms. The only thing he can do is to replace that form by another form. You can do something with temptation at its first stage. You can do everything with it. You can do a little with it at the second stage, but you can do nothing with it after it passes to the third stage. If you let it pass that, you are over Niagara. You must fight it, not by direct fight, but by flight to the higher regions. Paul summed it up in a single sentence, where he said: "Walk in the spirit, and ye shall not fulfill the lusts of the flesh." In plain English, walk in the fourth flat, and you will not do the things that people do in the cellar. You cannot be in two places at once. If you make up your mind to live continuously in the spirit, ye shall not fulfill the lusts of the flesh. Spirit is there contrasted with flesh. It does not mean primarily the Holy Spirit, although it includes that. It is here contrasted primarily with the flesh. Either live a cellar or a top-story life, a dog life or a man life. Walk among spiritual things, among high people—not necessarily religious things, but spiritual things. Look not on the things which are seen, but the things which are unseen. Be in the company of good books, beautiful pictures, and charming, delightful and inspiring music; and let all that one hears, sees, reads and thinks lift and inspire the higher. The man who does that is kept above the lower nature. Many and many a thing which is not directly religious, therefore, comes in to make up a part of the nourishment of the spiritual life.

We can always live a high life. We can always have before us beautiful, divine ideals, and the sudden attempt to get from the lower to the higher is the transition between the life of the flesh and the life of the spirit, and the passing from the one region into the other is done by a sudden act, by a sudden mental movement, by a transference of one's interests from one region to another. That mental movement, I think, may be dignified with the name of prayer. That sudden appeal to the purer image which is to displace the other and let it fade away is the spasmodic act of prayer, which instantly places one in the spiritual region; and that is one of the highest uses of prayer, not to get something directly from heaven, but to switch everything up, and not down. If you could keep a Christian and a God-like spirit, it would be impossible for you to have the lower appetites again.

If you want to get a man on his feet again, the thing to do is not to preach or read the Bible to him, but to get him out of the cellar in which he lives. Take him by the hand, and he will be led away from his former life. Those are psychological principles founded upon the fact that the attention cannot be directed to two things at the same moment. You see that, upon merely psychological principles, the man who understands his nature and applies that remedy for his case when he finds himself becoming a lower man than he ought to, is bound to get the victory. It is not by magic that men are able to succeed in living a high and Christian life. It is by living according to nature and according to the revelation of our higher nature. It is by living along the line of the laws under which this system of our human nature is founded. That is put in other words by Christ, where he says, "Abide in me"—the same thing on a still higher plane. The man who lives with Christ cannot sin. "If any man sin," John says, "he hath not known Christ." Sin is abashed in the presence of Christ. The man who lives in Christ as his ideal finds in Him a continuous living Saviour, drawing him away from himself and making it impossible for him to live for himself.

Let no man here to-night think or say that he can get victory over sin alone. He cannot get that out of religion unless he gets a great many other things as well, and is compelled to accept them. Deliverance from sin is only one of the functions of the new nature; and a man is not a new man if he has got only one arm. The one arm is to fight sin. He must be a full, perfect man; and the man who has simply got the muscle in his spiritual nature which is to deal with sin is not a Christian man at all necessarily. The man who attempts to live in one function alone will find it impossible. Religion is not a blue ribbon to wear against a single set of things. It is not an inoculation against a single disease. A man must accept Christ all around, not only as his Deliverer from sin, but as his friend and guide, his ideal and Saviour. He must walk his whole life, and every day of his life, in the spirit, not merely rushing into the top story when temptations are at his heels, but dwelling there, in that place where the air is always sweet, where the company is always pure, and where there is nothing to hinder the soul from communing with God and with the stars. If a man can continuously live in that region, he is bound to grow better and better. That is the picture of temptation chasing a man who walks in the Spirit. He hears its bark and feels its bite, like a dog's; but if he is off its ground it cannot touch him. Just in proportion as we live in the higher regions are we able to evade temptations.

In dealing with others, it is not enough to preach to them, to give them tracts, texts or prayers: but we must give them a new environment, in which the new nature can bud and flower and grow into perfection. Gentlemen, it is not such an easy business to save a man as some people think. It is not to be done by a few earnest words. That is why so many college men have been passed over untouched by our college Y. M. C. A.'s. It is not because we do not have meetings enough, not because we do not know the Bible well enough, not because we are not earnest enough; but it is because we do not proceed rationally enough. It is because we do not sow seeds for individuals and live so that they may be compelled to live this higher life with us. We do not do our work half thoroughly enough. Unless we lay down our lives to save men, we are not following the Master as we ought. It is good business to devote our lives to individuals. It may not be so picturesque, but individual work, where every man singles out his individual to help and save, and stands by him, if multiplied through the universities, would soon win our universities for Christ.

Make a continuous effort by will power and prayer power and the power of the Spirit of God to walk in the spiritual region; for nature abhors a vacuum. If we allow any pause to occur in our high living, if we leave this place, the enemy will come upon us, and we will be worse off after this Conference than we were before it.

The Kingdom of God and Your Part in it

"The futility of saving men by speech" is not a whole truth, but it is the large part of a truth. Imagine a life-saving crew trying to save wrecked mariners simply by calling to them, and not throwing out a life line or putting off in a boat after them! It is a case of life for life—a man laying down his own life for others, as Christ did.

In talking to a man you want to win, talk to him in his own language. If you want to get hold of an agnostic, try to translate what you have to say into simple words—words that will not be in every case the words in which you got it. It is not cant. Religion has its technical terms just as science, but it can be overdone; and, besides, it is an exceedingly valuable discipline for one's self. Take a text and say, "What does that mean in 19th century English ;" and in doing that you will learn the lesson that it is the spirit of truth that does one good, and not the form of words. The form does not matter, if it does you good and draws you nearer to God. Do not be suspicious of it, if it is God's truth, in whatever form it may be.

One has to do a great deal more than display his Christianity. He must not only talk it, but live it. What is the secret of Christianity? It is not picking out a man here and a man there and making them fit to go to heaven. Christ came to this world, as He Himself said, to found a society. Have you ever thought of that conception of Christianity? For hundreds of years it has been utterly lost sight of. It is only lately that men are getting to see the great Christian doctrine of the Kingdom of God. This great phrase was never off Christ's lips. "The Kingdom of God" is by far the commonest phrase in His speech. Have you ever given a month of your life to find out what Christ meant by "the Kingdom of God?" Every day as we pray, "Thy Kingdom come," has our Christian consciousness taken in the tremendous sweep of that prayer, and seen how it covers the length and breadth of this great world and every human being? Christ was continually telling what it was. The Kingdom of heaven is like unto this. The kingdom of heaven is like unto that. If there is one thing more prominent than another in Christ's language it is in explaining what the kingdom of heaven is, and in what the subjects of that kingdom are to busy themselves. The kingdom of God is a society for the best men working for the best end, with the highest motive according to the best principle. The Kingdom of God was to come without observation. Christ likened it to leaven, and one cannot get a better understanding of the meaning of His phrase than by taking His own metaphors. The world is sunken, Christ said, and it must be raised. Leaven comes from the same word as lever. It is that which lifts, elevates, or raises. Christ founded a society of men for the purpose of raising men. This leaven was not to disturb the form of or overturn any institution. When you put leaven into a vessel with anything that is to be leavened, it does not affect the outward form of it; but it changes its spirit.

The Kingdom of God is like leaven. It is to act, raising men by contagion, by the contact of one life with another. Did you ever put a little leaven under a microscope? If you did, you found it was a minute plant, perhaps one six-thousandth of an inch in diameter, with such an amazing power of propagation that, simply in contact with the dough, it has the effect of lifting it by means of the life that is in it. And so the virtue of the Christian's life, not by tempting it in the way of forcing it, but by its spontaneous, natural and beautiful goodness, reacts upon others. When men observe the fragrance of Christ and are reminded of Him, a longing comes over them to live like Him and breathe that air and have that calm, that beauty of character, and all that unconscious influence going out as a contagion to others. By these men the world is raised.

But that is not all. The world is not only sunken, it is sinful. Those of you who know life even an inch below the surface, know that even in this Christian country, in our great cities, the world is rotten. Have you ever thought of the sin of the world? Think of the sin in your own being. Think that the man in the next house has the same amount of sin in him, and all the people in your street are like that. Multiply that by the number of all the streets in your city, and that by the number of cities in your country, and that by the number of countries in the world, and you have a ghastly spectre under which your imagination staggers.

That, however, is only a single glimpse of this sinful world, for the sin can be taken away: "Behold the Lamb of God, which taketh away the sin of the world." How does He do it? By forgiving the sin of the world, and by taking it away, through you and me and other subjects of His kingdom.

Christians, the followers of Christ, He said, are the salt of the earth, and it is that salt that takes away the rottenness of the world. He takes away the guilt and the power of it, and you help Him to remove it by being salt in the society in which you live. Salt is that which keeps society from becoming rotten. You put salt upon fish or meat to prevent it from becoming rotten; and it is the Christian men and women in this country who prevent it from becoming absolutely rotten. Christianity is the great antiseptic of society. If you were to take Christianity out of New York, Chicago, Berlin, or Paris, those cities, in a few generations, would go to pieces, even physically, and be swept off the earth. Now, we are to be the salt of Chicago, New York and the great cities of the world. It is our business to make cities and to keep those cities sweet—not only to scavenge away the rottenness after it has grown there, but to prevent the new generation that is growing up from becoming rotten. The work of salt is to prevent this, as well as to cure it. Keep those children pure to the end of their lives. We do not emphasize half enough the prevention side of Christian society. We do not emphasize half enough the making of Christian environment in which a Christ-like life shall be possible—new

houses, pure air and water, good schools, bringing the influences of
sweetest life and purity to keep those young lives from succumbing to the
influences which surround them. The world which you and I have to lift
is not only the world of the poor; but we have to lift up our country.

One thing, gentlemen, strikes the stranger in coming to this country.
He goes to a city like Boston, and finds the merchants of that city with
their heads buried in their ledgers, wholly occupied with their private
business, while a few Irishmen, holding the city offices, are carrying on
their municipal government. Some one has defined dirt as matter in the
wrong place; and it is matter in the wrong place for a company of
Irishmen to regulate the affairs of the city of Boston. Therefore,
gentlemen, if you are the subjects of the Kingdom of God, you must give
to the world and to your country a reformed Boston, a reformed Chicago,
above all a reformed New York. You have been taught in your schools of
your duties as citizens; but you are taught in this Book just as plainly
your duties as Christian citizens. These cities are making the people that
are living in them. People will not be righteous. In this country there is
not only little honesty and honorableness in municipal life; but, what is
a thousand times worse, there is little in its possibility. In my country I
have never known or heard of a member of the government, either
municipal or state, proving false to his trust. It is your duty to restore
righteousness in the high places of this government. Let the people see
examples which will help them in their Christian life. I cannot speak too
strongly about that, because I know that the thing in process of time can
be done. We have had rotten municipal government, and the Christian
men of the place have taken the thing up and said, we have determined
this shall not be. In the old cities, they have put man after man into the
municipal chair simply because they were Christian men, because they
would deal with the people righteously, and carry out the programme of
Christianity for the city. Let me tell you of the work of some university
men in the city of London. They went to a district in the East End—a
God-forsaken and sunken place, occupied for miles entirely by working
people. They rented a house and became known as settlers in that poor
district. They gave themselves no airs of superiority. They did not tell the
people they had come to do them good. They went in there and made
friends with the people. The leaven went in among the dough. The salt
went in beside that which was corrupt. We keep the grains of salt all
together, and the other things all together; but the very place where the
salt ought not to be is beside the salt. It ought to be scattered over the
meat. Well, these men were not in a great hurry. They waited some
months and got to know a number of the workmen, and got to understand
one another. They had studied the city, and the workingmen were
astonished at how much the young fellows knew about city government,
city life and education, and sanitation, cleansing and purity in all
directions. One day there came a great war of labor. The working men put
their heads together and said, "These young fellows have heads. Let us go
and talk the matter over with them." In a few months those young men
were the arbiters of a strike, and at a single word from them three or four

thousand families were saved from being thrown out of work on a great strike. Is that not a Christian thing to do? If you understand the conception of the Kingdom of God as a society of the best men working for the best ends for the amelioration of human life, you will agree with me. One of these young men at the next election was elected a member of one of the municipal boards, and in a few months he was the head of the Board. Another got into the School Board, and in a short time was the head of it. These men did not claim to be superior. They were elected kings by the people because the people felt their kingship. By and by the time came when a member of Parliament was to be returned. The workingmen came again to their university friends and said, ``Whom shall we put in?'' Those men told them, and they put him in. And so those men have taken possession of that city in the name of Jesus Christ, and have been gradually working, leavening and salting. First, the blade; then, the ear; and then, the full corn in the ear.

It is coming without observation. It is not the work of a day. Christians are the only agents God has for carrying out His purposes. Think of that. He could Himself, with a single breath, cleanse the whole of London or New York, but he does not do it. It is by the members of His body that he carries on His work. We all have different parts of that work to do. Some of us are thumbs, some of us are fingers, and some of us are only a little bit of the little finger. Some, again, are limbs.

Now, that conception of Christianity as a kingdom is beginning to grow throughout Christendom at this hour. Every age has had its peculiar side of Christianity emphasized; and the side that is being emphasized now is the social side, that large conception of what Christ came to do, how He came to save men in the bulk, as it were —by the city and by the country; and many of the movements that are going on just now in society, in education, in sanitation, in university extension and philanthropy, are all working together for good in that direction. Let not us, who believe in the salvation of the individual soul as the supreme thing, shut our eyes to the Christianity of Christ, to His great conception of the Kingdom of God.

All the activities of Christianity may be classed under one or the other of these two heads—entering the kingdom of God ourselves, and spreading it to the lives of others. The individual life has been at this Conference. How is it to help on this movement for the bringing of the world to Christ? I know many of you are puzzled to know in what direction you can start off to help Christ. Let me simply say this to you. Once in my own life I came to crossroads. I did not know in which direction God wanted me to help His kingdom, and I started to read this Book to find out what the ideal life was. I knew I had only one life, and didn't want to miss it; and I found out that the only thing worth doing in the world was to do the will of God. Whether that was done in the pulpit or in the slums, whether done in the college class room or in the street, didn't matter at all. "My meat and my drink," Christ said, "is to do the will of Him that sent me;" and if you make up your mind to do the will of God, it matters little in what direction. There are more posts waiting for men than there are men waiting for posts. Christ needs men in every

community and in every land. It makes little difference whether we go to
foreign lands or stay at home, so it is where Gods puts us. I am not jealous
of the great missionary movement which has swept this country. In my
own college, at least one third of the men are going to the foreign mission
field. I am not jealous of that movement. I rejoice in it. But I should like
also to bid for men, both for my country and for yours, men who will give
their lives to the Kingdom of God at home.

You will say, "How am I to know whether to go abroad or stay at home,
be a lawyer or a Christian doctor?" The first thing is, course. The second
thing is, think. Think over all the different lines of work—over all your
own pray, of qualifications. If you are called to the missionary field, think
of all the different kinds of missionary fields. There are some that do not
need you at all; and there are others for which you are the very man. It is
a great mistake to suppose that missionary fields are all alike, and that
they are the same in Africa as in India or China. They are not the same
at all. Study the field. The third thing is, regard his decision as final.
Nobody can plan your life for you. Do take the advice of a wise friend, but
do not not imagine that the most disagreeable of two or three alternative
things before you is necessarily the will of God.

God's will does not always lie in the line of the disagreeable. God likes
to see His children happy just as earthly fathers like to see their children
happy, and there may be plums waiting for you as well as stones. Do not
sacrifice to a thing that is disagreeable unless you are quite sure it is
God's will.

The next thing is, when the time of decision comes, what light you have.
We do not manufacture a act, go ahead with decision out of all these
elements. We arrive at a decision. Some day, in a turn of the road, we find
we are led. We do not know how. The subject just took shape in our minds
somehow, and we arrived at a decision.

Having once decided, the next thing is, never reconsider your decision.
The day after a man makes a great life's decision, if he reconsiders it, he
reverses it. Never reconsider such a decision. You will never know for
months or years whether you have done the right thing; but then, you will
see that God has led every step of your way. One good general rule is to
go in the direction of least resistance, if you find objections in every line
and there is no one line positively drawing you out.

I want to return to the immediate purpose of those of you who are not
yet out in the mission field, but who have a year or two at college before
you. I ask you to study what Christianity is, and to spread the knowledge
of that through your university. There are many men in the universities
who do not know in the least what Christianity is. When I was in the
university I thought Christianity was a thing you might put on the point
of a needle, and that Jesus Christ was a being so small that you had to
search closely for Him before you found Him; and now I know the whole
earth is full of His glory. Study the Kingdom of God. See what Christ said
was life, and how the members of that kingdom are to pass it on to others,
to the lawyer and the doctor, until we have the professions Christianized,

and the whole country will follow. It begins with you. Give your life for a life.

I will close with a specific case of one of your own countrymen. One night I got a letter from one of the students in the University of Edinburgh, with page after page of agnosticism and atheism. I went to see him, and spent a whole afternoon with him, but did not make the slightest impression. At Edinburgh University we have a students' evangelistic meeting Sunday nights, with an attendance of 800 or 1,000 men. A few nights after my conversation with this young man I saw him at one of these meetings. Beside him sat a man I had seen occasionally at the meetings, but whose name I did not know. After the meeting I spoke to the latter student and asked him if he knew the man sitting next to him. He said: "I am a graduate. After I finished my regular course of study, I wanted to take a post-graduate course; and last year I came to Edinburgh, where, in the dissecting room, I happened to be placed near this man. I took a singular liking to him. I found out he was not a religious man. A year passed without any change in him. I went to pack my trunks to go home at the end of my one year's post-graduate work; but I was uncertain whether I should go and take up my profession in America, or stay in Edinburgh and try to win that one man for Christ. I decided I would stay." "Well," I said, "my young fellow, it will pay you. You will get your man." Two or three months passed. It came to the night for our students' farewell meeting—a service some of you might well imitate. We have men in Edinburgh University from every part of the world. Every year five or six hundred of them go out never to meet again. In our religious work we get very close to one another; and on the last night of the university year we sit down together in our common hall to the Lord's Supper. This is entirely a students' meeting; but that night the members of the Theological Faculty participate, so that things may be done decently and in order. There you see hundreds of men—the cream and the youth of the world—sitting down to the Lord's table, many of them not members of the church, there for the first time pledging themselves to become members of the Kingdom of God. I saw one, sitting down, passing the communion cup to his American friend. The American had won the agnostic for Christ. A week after, he was back to his own country. I do not know his name, but he was a subject of Christ's Kingdom doing his Master's work. A few weeks passed, and the friend he rescued from agnosticism came to see me and said: "I want to tell you that I am going to be a medical missionary."

Before you leave here, make up your mind that, with God's help, you will try to land your man. Let us ask God to use us in His work.

The Three Elements of a Complete Life

Students are very often recommended to invest in certain books. I am going to take the liberty of suggesting to some of you to buy a certain picture which you can get for a very few cents. Most of you have already seen it. It is "The Angelus." It is an illuminated text. God speaks through you. He also speaks through art. I want to hang up this picture as an illuminated text. There are three things in the picture—a potato field, a country lad and a country girl standing on the ground, and on the far horizon the spire of the village church. That is the whole thing. There is no great scenery, no picturesque scenery; just a country lad and a country girl. In those Roman Catholic countries, at the hour of evening, the church bell rings out to summon the people to pray. Some go into the church to pray; and those that are caught in the fields when the Angelus rings bow their heads to engage for a few moments in silent prayer.

Now, that picture is a perfect picture of Christian life; and what is interesting about it is that it picks out the three great pedestals of life. Moody said it was not enough to have the root of the matter, we must have the whole thing.

I

The first element in life is work Three-fourths of our life is probably spent in work. Is that religious, or is it not? What is the meaning of it? It means, of course, that our work is just as religious as our worship; and unless we can make our work religious, three-fourths of our life remains unsanctified. The proof that work is religious is that the most of Christ's life was spent in work. It was not the Bible that was in His hands during these first thirty years of His life. It was the hammer and the plane. He was making chairs and tables and plows and yokes. That is to say, the highest conceivable life is in doing work. Christ's public ministry occupied only two and a half years. The great bulk of His time, He was simply at work; and from that moment work has had a new meaning given to it. When Christ came into the world He came to men at their work. He appealed to the shepherds, the working classes of those days. He also appealed to the wise men, the students of those days. Three deputations of the world went out to welcome him—first, the shepherds; second, the wise men; third, two old people, Simeon and Anna, in the temple. That is to say, Christ comes to men at their work, as the shepherds. He comes to men at their books—the wise men. He comes to men at their worship—Simeon and Anna. We find Christ, therefore, at our work, our books and our worship. But you will notice that it was the old people who found Christ at their worship, and, as we get older, we will cease to find Christ so much at our work and our books. We will then spend more of our time in worship than we are able to now, and as we get old we will repair to the prayer meeting and the House of God and meet Christ and worship Him as Simeon and Anna. We must try, until the time comes when much of our time shall be given to direct business, to find Christ in our books and at our common work.

Why should God have arranged that so many hours of every day should be occupied with work? It is because work makes men. A university is not a place for making scholars. It is a place for making Christians. A farm is not a place for growing grain. It is a place for growing character, and a man has no character except what is built up through the medium of the things he does from day to day. God's Spirit aids it through the actions which he performs during his life-work. The student turns up every word in his Latin, instead of consulting the translation. The result is that honesty is translated into the student's being. If he gets up his mathematics thoroughly he not only becomes a mathematician and a learned man, but he becomes a thorough man. If he attends to the instructions that are given to him in class intelligently and conscientiously he becomes a conscientious man, and it is just by such means that thoroughness, conscientiousness and honorableness are imbedded in our being. We do not get perfect character in our sleep. It comes to us as muscle comes, through doing things. It is the muscle of the soul, and it comes by exercising it upon actual things. Hence the meaning of our work is that it is the making of us, and it is only by and through our work that the great Christian graces are communicated to our souls. That is the means God requires for the growing of the Christian principles. We cannot have Christian character unless we use these means. Hence, gentlemen, the necessity of a student being true, first of all, to his work, and letting his Christianity show itself to his fellow students and his professors by the integrity and the thoroughness of his academic work. Unless he is faithful in that which is least, it is impossible for him to be faithful in that which is much. The world judges a student by the conscientiousness and faithfulness with which he does his college work. I know men who were led to pass their examinations simply because they had become Christians—men who struggled for years to pass their examinations, but who, when they became Christians, got to work and succeeded where they had previously failed. Christianity comes out in a man as much in his work as in his worship. Our work is not only to be done thoroughly, but it is to be done honestly. In dealing with that august thing called truth a man must be square with himself, fair to his own mind and to the principles and spirit of truth. We are students, and it is our business to get to the bottom of difficulties. Perhaps some truths which are revealed to us have deeper bottoms than we now know. We will get down to nuggets if we go below the surface, as our chairman said this morning. Christianity is the most important thing in the world, and the student ought to sound it in every direction and see if there is deep water and a safe place through which to steer his life. If there are shoals, he ought to know them. Therefore, when we come to difficulties, let us not be guilty of intellectual sin, jumping lightly over them. Let us be honest seekers after truth. We do not ask the public to sift doctrines, but it is the business of the student to exercise the intellect which God has given him. Faith is never opposed to reason in the New Testament. It is often supposed to be so, but it is not. Faith is opposed to sight, but never to reason. It is only by reason that we can sift and examine and criticise, and be sure of the forms of truth which are given us as Christians. Hence a great field of work has opened to the student even apart from his academic work. Let him be sure that in seeking after truth he is drawing very near Christ. "I am the way, the truth and the life." We talk a great deal about Christ as the way and about Christ as the life; but there is a side of Christ especially for the student, "I am the truth." Every student ought to be a truth-learner and a truth-seeker for Christ's sake.

II

The second element in life after work—and it ought to be put first in importance—is God. The Angelus is perhaps the most religious picture painted in this century. You cannot look at it and see that young man standing in the field with his hat off, and the girl opposite him with her hands clasped and her head bowed on her breast, without feeling a sense of God. Gentlemen, do we carry about with us wherever we go a sense of God? If not, we have missed the greatest part of life. Do we have that feeling and conviction of God's abiding presence wherever we are? Does He beset us behind and before? There is nothing more needed in this generation than a larger and more scriptural idea of God. A great American writer has told us that the conception of God that he got, in books and from sermons, when he was a boy, was that of a wise and very strict lawyer sitting in his office. I remember very well the awful conception I got when I was a boy. I was given a book of Watts' hymns, which was illustrated, and, amongst other hymns, there was one about God, and it represented a great black, scowling thunder cloud, and in the midst of that cloud there was a piercing eye. That was placed before my young imagination as God, and I got the idea that God was a great detective, playing the spy upon my actions, and, as the hymn says, writing now the story of what little children do. That was a bad lesson. It has taken years to obliterate it. We think of God as "up there." You know there is no such thing as "up there." What would be "up there" tonight will be "down there" twelve hours from this time. Do not think of God as "up there," because there is no such place. Science has been "up there," and it has not seen God. You say God made the world six thousand years ago and then He retired. That is the last that was seen of Him. He made the world and then went away into space somewhere to look on and keep things going. Geology has been away back there, and God has gone further and further back. These six thousand years have extended back into ages and ages of long, long years. Where is God, if He is not back there in time or up there in space? Where is He? God is in you. The Kingdom of God is within you and God Himself is within men. He is not "up there." When are we to exchange the terrible God of our childhood, the far-away God of our childhood, for the everywhere-present God of the Bible?

The God of theology has been largely taken from the old classical Christian-Roman writers, such as Augustine, who, great as they were, had nothing better to fling their conception of God upon than that of the greatest man. The greatest man was the Roman emperor, and therefore God became a kind of emperor. The Greeks had a far grander conception—the conception of Clement of Alexandria, which is coming again into modern theology. The Greek God is the God of this Book; the Spirit which moved upon the water; the God in whom we live and move and have our being; the God of whom Jesus spake to the woman at the well; the God who is a spirit. God is a spirit. Let us gather the conception of the immanent God. That is the theological word for it, and it is a splendid word. Immanuel, God with us, the inside God, the immanent God. You have had singular experiences since you have been here. What is it? It is God working in you. Have we really realized that God is in us and is working in us? God must be working in us. Long, long ago God made matter. Then He made flowers, trees and animals. Then he made man. Did He stop? Is God dead? If He lives, if He acts, what is He doing? He is making better men. He is carrying on the development of man. "It is God which worketh in you." The buds of our nature are not all out yet. The sap to make them come out comes from God, from the indwelling immanent Christ. Our bodies, therefore, are the temples of the Holy Ghost. We must bear Christ with us wherever we go, because the sense of God is not kept up by logic but by experience.

Most of you have heard of Hellen Kellar, the Boston girl who is deaf and dumb and blind. Until she was seven years of age her mind was an absolute blank. Nothing could get into that blank, because all the avenues to the other world were closed. Then, by that great process which Boston has discovered, by which the blind see, the deaf hear and the mute speak, that girl's soul was opened. Bit by bit they began to build up a mind —to give her a certain amount of information and to educate her. But no one liked to tell her about religion. They reserved that for Phillips Brooks. After some years had passed they took her to him and he began to talk to her, through the young lady who had been the means of opening her senses, and was able to communicate with her by the delicate process of touch. Phillips Brooks began to tell her about God, who God was, what He had done, how He loved men and what He was to us. The child listened very intently. Then she looked up and said: "Mr. Brooks, I knew all that before, but I didn't know His name." There was some mysterious pressure, some impelling power, some guide, some elevating impulse, within her soul. "It is *God*," said Phillips Brooks, "which worketh in you. God is with us and in us."

I wonder if you have heard the story of the two Americans who were once crossing the Atlantic and met in the cabin on Sunday night to sing hymns. As they sang the last hymn, "Jesus, Lover of my Soul," one of them heard an exceedingly rich and beautiful voice behind him. He looked around, and, although he did not know the face, he thought that he knew the voice. So, when the music ceased, he turned and asked the man if he had been in the Civil War.

The man replied that he had been a Confederate soldier.

"Were you at such a place at such a night?" asked the first.

"Yes," he replied, "and a curious thing happened that night which this hymn has recalled to my mind. I was posted on sentry duty near the edge of a wood. It was a dark night and very cold, and I was a little frightened because the enemy were supposed to be very near. About midnight, when everything was very still and I was feeling homesick and miserable and weary, I thought that I would comfort myself by praying and singing a hymn. I remember singing this hymn:

" `All my trust on Thee is stayed,
All my help from Thee I bring;
Cover my defenseless head
With the shadow of Thy wing.'

"After singing that a strange peace came down upon me, and through the long night I felt no more fear."

"Now," said the other, "listen to my story. I was a Union soldier and was in the wood that night with a party of scouts. I saw you standing, although I did not see your face. My men had their rifles focused upon you, waiting the word to fire, but when you sang out:

" `Cover my defenseless head
With the shadow of Thy wing'

I said: `Boys, lower your rifles; we will go home.' It was God working in each of them. Just by such means, by this everywhere-acting, mysterious spirit, God keeps His Spirit moving. Hence that second great element in life, *God*, without Whom life is a living death.

III

A moment or two about the third element in life. The first is "work," the second is "God," the third is "love." You have noticed in that picture the sense of companionship, brought out by the young man and the young woman. It matters not whether they are brother and sister or lover and lover. There you have the idea of friendship, the final ingredient in our lives. If the man had been standing in that field alone, the scene would be almost weary. If the woman had been standing alone it would have been sentimental. You can carry much away from this Conference; but we can all carry away with us some enrichment of our human friendship, and that will complete our life, because no life is complete unless it has that additional element in it. That, after all, is the divine element in life, because God is love and because he that loveth is born of God. Therefore, gentlemen, after we leave one another, let us keep our friendships in repair, as some one says. They are worth while spending time on and keeping them up, because they constitute a large part of our life. I need not say that we must cultivate this spirit of friendship and let it grow into a great love not only for our friends, but for all humanity. Some of you are going into the mission field. Your mission field will be a failure unless you cultivate this element. Two years ago I was wandering about the coral islands of the Pacific, and I came to one island far remote from human gaze, inhabited solely by cannibals. At one end of the island was a missionary and his wife. At the other end of the island was another missionary and his wife. They never heard from other parts of the world for six months. You would suppose they would see each other every day, but they were not on loving terms. They were not on speaking terms. They were on war terms. One had actually assaulted the other. What was the trouble about? It was a quarrel over the word in the native language they should use for "God" in their translation of the New Testament. They needed and lacked charity, tenderness, tolerance, patience.

So these three things—work, God, love—form a complete life. If your life is not comfortable, if you are ill at ease, ask yourself if you are not lacking in one or other of these three things, and pray for them and work for them.

www.ingramcontent.com/pod-product-compliance
Lightning Source LLC
Chambersburg PA
CBHW061756040426
42447CB00011B/2325